Taking Control of Your Career

STEP BY STEP GUIDE TO JOB SEARCH

Dave Yancey

Copyright © 2024 Dave Yancey

All rights reserved.

No portion of this book may be reproduced in any form without written permission from the publisher or author except as permitted by U.S. copyright law.

This publication is designed to provide accurate and authoritative information in regard to the subject matter covered. It is sold with the understanding that neither the author nor the publisher is engaged in rendering legal, investment, accounting, or other professional services. While the publisher and author have used their best efforts in preparing this book, they make no representations or warranties with respect to the accuracy or completeness of the contents of this book and specifically disclaim any implied warranties of merchantability or fitness for a particular purpose. No warranty may be created or extended by sales representatives or written sales materials. The advice and strategies contained herein may not be suitable for your situation. You should consult with a professional when appropriate. Neither the publisher nor the author shall be liable for any loss of profit or any other commercial damages, including but not limited to special, incidental, consequential, personal, or other damages.

Independently Published
ISBN-13: 9798329818406 - Paperback
ISBN-13: 9798329918144 – Hardcover

Introduction

Now, I'm sure you are asking yourself why there is yet another book on how to find a job. Well, the answer is simple. As of this writing, I have found myself looking for a new job, and so I had a wild thought, "Hey Dave, why don't you write a book about the process you go through in finding a job since it's top of mind." So, of course, I must answer myself, so I did, "Sure, Dave, I think that's a great idea."

Let's face it—finding a job is daunting, especially in today's ever-evolving job market. Whether you are a recent graduate stepping into the professional world for the first time, a seasoned professional seeking new challenges, or someone facing the challenges of finding a new job, understanding the intricacies of career management is crucial for success.

This book aims to guide you through the process, providing you with the tools and knowledge to start the process and manage your job search effectively. Each chapter offers practical advice, proven strategies, and real-world examples to help you along the journey and, hopefully, the job you desire.

The Tools

In the first chapter, we will outline the tools you need to succeed in your journey. These tools include your resume, recruiters, job search tracking, and attitude.

Crafting a Resume

Your resume is your personal marketing tool. Discover the fundamentals of crafting a compelling resume that showcases your skills, experiences, and accomplishments, ensuring that you stand out to potential employers.

Tailoring a Resume

One size does not fit all when it comes to resumes. Here, we discuss the importance of tailoring your resume for different job applications and provide tips on aligning your resume with specific job descriptions to increase your chances of getting noticed.

Working with Recruiters

Recruiters can be valuable allies in your job search. Providing insights into effectively collaborating with recruiters, understanding their role in the hiring process, and leveraging their expertise to find the right job opportunities.

How to Handle Different Interview Styles

Interviews can be nerve-wracking, but preparation is vital. We explore various interview styles, from traditional to behavioral to case interviews, and how to prepare for the most common of these styles.

Common Interview Questions

What are the most common interview questions? This chapter will discuss the fifteen most common questions and strategies for answering them confidently and effectively.

Negotiating an Offer

Receiving a job offer is exciting, but negotiating terms can be challenging. This chapter guides you through the negotiation process, helping you to secure the best possible terms and ensuring that your compensation and benefits align with your expectations.

Accepting the Offer

Once you have negotiated your offer, it's time to accept it formally. We discuss the steps involved in accessing and finally deciding to accept a job offer, from understanding the contract details to communicating your acceptance professionally.

Handling Rejection

Rejection is a natural part of the job search process. Here, we provide strategies for coping with rejection, learning from the experience, and maintaining a positive outlook as you continue your job search.

Exiting Your Current Job

Leaving a job can be just as significant as starting a new one. In the final chapter, we discuss how to best approach leaving your position, whether you were terminated, laid off, or left voluntarily. We also discuss leaving on the best terms and not following social media trends for your departure.

Final Thoughts

Each Chapter will include final thoughts summarizing what was discussed or outlined. By the end of this book, you will have a comprehensive understanding of the career management process and be equipped with the skills and knowledge to navigate each stage successfully. Your career is a journey, and with the right strategies and mindset, you can confidently steer it towards a fulfilling and rewarding future.

ONE

The Tools

Embarking on the job-hunting journey is a familiar path that I've trodden on several times. However, my recent experience has prompted me to reflect on the process, which has almost become second nature. I invite you to join me as I share these valuable insights and strategies that have proven successful in my job hunts.

Let me make something clear before we jump into the process. As an Agile/Technical Coach, I am often on short-term contracts and, therefore, looking for new engagements. Because of this, I have worked out a process that helps me stay focused and in charge of my career.

The core of any process or system is your tools. In job hunting, your resume or curriculum vitae are like your trusted companions. They are core to your process, but just as when you go out hunting for a deer or duck, you bring more than your gun or ammo; you need more than your resume.

Resume

Your résumé, often spelled as Resume, is a critical player in your job-hunting process. It's a summary of your background, skills, and accomplishments, a digital representation of your professional identity. Depending on the type of position you are applying for, a resume may be accompanied by a cover letter.

The curriculum vitae, Latin for 'course of life,' may be used in place of the resume. It is generally a shorter, more concise version of the resume and is used predominantly in the UK and other European countries. In the next chapter, we'll discuss crafting your resume more in-depth.

LinkedIn / Job Boards

Twenty years ago, your resume, printed in multiple copies, would have been sufficient for you to carry with you on your hunt. With the advances in technology and web applications, LinkedIn has become a valuable tool to keep in your bag. Think of LinkedIn as a networking platform where your visible profile is your resume.

LinkedIn also features a job search for recruiters and candidates; you should create profiles on other job boards, such as Indeed and Dice.

Recruiters

Recruiters can be as important to you on your job hunt as an agent is to an athlete. They are the connection between you and the company, maintaining a view of what the market is doing and the skills required for the different roles that are available or 'hot.' Chapter 3 will cover tips on choosing a recruiter and how to work with your recruiters.

Tracker

One of the most valuable tools to have with you on your hunt is a way to track your process. For my hunt, I use a spreadsheet that lets me keep track of the role, company, contact, status, date, and any notes for the roles I have applied for. Your tracker is as crucial to your hunt as your resume is.

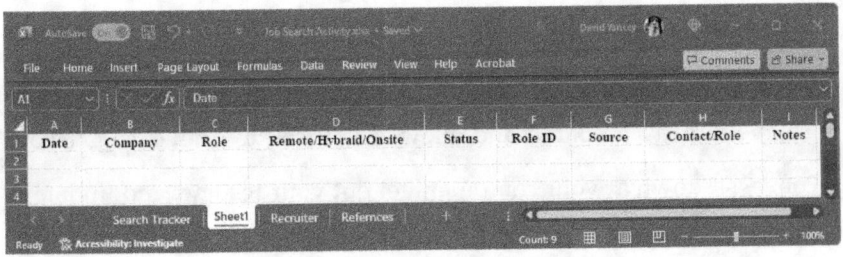

Attitude

Having a positive attitude while challenging is critical when on the hunt. When you receive the news that you are being sent out, learn to take the gems and discard the rest. Learn what you can from the termination or layoff. An example of this could be that the reason for a layoff is that the position was eliminated. It would be easy to take it personally, and you may at first think. However, changing your viewpoint and accepting that this is real and you were not at fault will give you a better leg up on your search. There will be times when you are terminated, and it is due to something that you did. This is where you 'take the gems,' or in other words, those lessons you can learn from and grow from. The rest, discard. *Set your attitude correctly*.

The Preparation

As you begin the job hunt, you must allow yourself to grieve for whatever brought you to this point of needing a job hunt. Allow yourself to get mad, cry, and take a day. Keep it at one day; you don't want to allow yourself to 'live' in this state of grief. So, the following day, it is time to get up, get busy, and get hunting.

The Hunt

Day One

On day one, the first thing you need to do is gather your tools. You've already prepared and allowed yourself to grieve, so get your coffee, sit down at your computer, get out your resume, and update it. While updating and reviewing your resume, work on your list of recruiters you have a relationship with and contact them, letting them know you are on the market. If you don't have any that you have a good relationship with, then now is the best time to start building those relationships. You will also want to understand what your next position looks like regarding responsibilities and salary expectations.

Now that you have updated your list and resume, you will want to send them to your recruiters along with any other information they requested. Next, create your tracker. I always create a new one to help me stay focused on the current hunt and not get distracted from previous hunts.

Your final task for Day One is to update your LinkedIn profile. Just as with your resume, ensure that you have it updated with your most recent experience and details describing your responsibilities. You are also advised to use the 'Open to' feature in LinkedIn to let your network and recruiters who use the platform know that you are open to new opportunities.

Day Onward

Each day onward starts with browsing job postings on the job boards. Look at the details of any position that interests you. Take notes of requirements, such as education, skill sets, and experience. If you see any skills you have that are not on your resume, this would be an excellent time to update your resume again. Remember that this will be a process you will frequently come back to as you find roles, and work with your recruiter to find possible roles. As you update your resume, send the updated version to your recruiters. Work with them by following recommendations to fine-tune your resume. Remember, you work with them because they are in touch with what the market is looking for.

When your recruiter finds a role they want to submit you to, they will work with you, adjust your resume for that position, and give you details such as requirements, company, compensation packages, etc. For each role they submit you to, you will want to log that in your tracker. This is critical as it will help ensure you are not submitted to the same role more than once. As you are finding positions on the job boards, if you submit your resume yourself, log it in your tracker. Be sure to note who your contact is, if you have a name, and where you found that position, whether it is on a job board such as LinkedIn or the job board for a company directly.

Final Thoughts

As mentioned earlier, maintaining a positive attitude is key to your success during the job search. It's normal to feel frustrated as you apply for roles and wait for responses. Use your tracker to plan your follow-up emails or calls. When you secure an interview, make sure you're well-prepared beforehand. Collaborate with your recruiter or the company's recruiter to increase your chances of success.

Remember, finding a new job is a process that requires dedication and patience. Be kind to yourself and the process. Stay open to feedback, be willing to modify your resume, and be prepared to make appropriate compromises. This approach will help you stay focused and adaptable during your job search.

TWO

Crafting a Compelling Resume

Creating a strong resume is essential in the job search process. It is your personal marketing tool, designed to showcase your skills, experience, and accomplishments to potential employers. A well-crafted resume can open doors, spark interest, and possibly lead to that coveted interview.

Your resume introduces you to potential employers; it is a networking tool. Your resume demonstrates to recruiters and hiring managers which roles you may be a fit for quickly—highlighting your relevant skills and experiences and determining which ones may align with the skills and experience they are looking for. A well-crafted resume should pique the employer's interest, prompting them to invite you for a conversation.

Step-by-Step Guide to Crafting a Resume

Step 1: Choose the Right Format

There are three main resume formats: chronological, functional, and combination. Each serves a different purpose and is suited to different types of job seekers. The chronological resume will lay out your work experience in reverse chronological order and is ideal for those with a solid work history. The functional resume focuses on skills and experiences rather than chronological work history; you will want to choose this format if you are starting on your first hunt or if you happen to have gaps in your job history. The combination resume blends the chronological and functional formats, highlighting skills while providing a detailed work history, making it suitable for those with extensive experience and transferable skills.

Step 2: Write a Strong Header

Your resume's header should include your full legal name, phone number, email address, LinkedIn profile, and personal website, if applicable. Ensure that your contact information is up-to-date. If you don't have a professional email address, preferably including your name, then you will want to create one. If you have a preferred name, then include that in your header just under your legal name.

Example:

John Doe

(123) 456-7890

john.doe@example.com

linkedin.com/in/johndoe

Step 3: Craft a Compelling Summary

The summary section is a brief statement that encapsulates your professional identity and career goals. It should be tailored to the job you are applying for and highlight your most relevant qualifications and achievements.

Example:

Marketing professional with over ten years of experience developing and executing innovative marketing strategies that drive brand awareness, customer engagement, and revenue growth. With a proven track record in managing multi-channel campaigns, leveraging data analytics to optimize performance, and leading cross-functional teams to achieve organizational goals. I am seeking new opportunities with an organization, collaborating with a forward-thinking team, taking on new challenges within the marketing landscape, and learning while contributing to continued success and driving new growth.

Step 4: Detail Your Professional Experience

This is where you will list your work experience in reverse chronological order. For each position, include the job title, company name, location, and dates of employment. Describe your responsibilities concisely and highlight key achievements using active verbs and quantifiable metrics where possible. Active verbs make your achievements sound more dynamic, while quantifiable metrics provide concrete evidence of your success.

Example:

Senior Software Developer

Tech Solutions, San Francisco, CA

June 2019 – Present

- Led a team of 5 developers to create a new e-commerce

platform, increasing online sales by 30%.
- Implemented Agile processes, reducing project delivery times by 15%.
- Developed a customer feedback system using React and Node.js, enhancing user satisfaction by 25%.

Step 5: Showcase Your Education

List your educational background, including degrees earned, institutions attended, and graduation dates. You may also include relevant coursework, honors, or certifications that pertain to the job you are seeking.

Example:

Bachelor of Science in Computer Science

University of California, Berkeley

Graduated: May 2018

Step 6: Highlight Skills and Certifications

Create a section to list your technical skills, soft skills, and any certifications that are relevant to the job. Be specific about your proficiency levels and include industry-standard terminology. Include this section for all resumes, including those not of a technical focus. Here are some examples to help you better understand how to list these skills.

Example:

Technical Skills:
- Software: Microsoft Office, Salesforce, Microsoft Dynamics, Peoplesoft
- Programming Languages: JavaScript, Python, Java

- Frameworks: React, Angular, Node.js
- Databases: MySQL, MongoDB
- Tools: Git, Docker, Jenkins

Certifications:
- Certified ScrumMaster (CSM)
- AWS Certified Solutions Architect

Step 7: Include Additional Sections

Depending on your background and the job you are applying for, you might include additional sections such as certifications, projects, publications, volunteer work, or professional affiliations. These sections can provide a complete picture of your capabilities and interests and demonstrate your initiative, creativity, and commitment.

Example:

Projects:
- Developed a real-time chat application using Socket.io and Node.js, which supports over 10,000 concurrent users.
- Created a machine learning model to predict customer churn for a SaaS company, achieving 85% accuracy.

Volunteer Work:
- Volunteer Coding Instructor at Code for Good, teaching programming basics to high school students.

Final Thoughts

Use keywords from the job description and focus on relevant experiences to make your resume stand out to potential employers. Proofread thoroughly to ensure there are no spelling or grammatical errors.

A well-proofread resume demonstrates attention to detail, which is crucial for making a positive impression. Keep your resume concise, aiming for a length of one to two pages, depending on your experience level. Be succinct and avoid unnecessary details to maintain the reader's interest. Let your resume be a conversation starter.

THREE

Tailoring your Resume

The job market is highly competitive, and employers often receive hundreds of applications for a single role. In such a competitive field, a generic resume that broadly showcases your skills and experiences is unlikely to make a strong impression. To stand out, you will want to present a resume tailored to the specific role you are applying for.

Why Tailoring Your Resume is Crucial

A tailored resume demonstrates your relevance to the role. It shows that you clearly understand the job requirements and how your skills and experiences align with them. This approach signals to the employer that you have done your homework and are genuinely interested in the position.

Additionally, a tailored resume captures attention quickly. Recruiters and hiring managers often spend only a few seconds scanning each resume. A tailored resume will stand out from the generic ones by including relevant keywords and clearly highlighting relevant experiences, thus increasing your chances of advancing to the next stage.

Customizing your resume also allows you to highlight your strengths. By emphasizing the aspects of your background most pertinent to the role, you can differentiate yourself from other candidates who may have similar qualifications but fail to showcase their relevance effectively.

Finally, tailoring your resume will help you pass through the Applicant Tracking Systems (ATS). Many companies use these systems to filter resumes before they reach human reviewers. Incorporating the right keywords and phrases increases your resume's likelihood of successfully navigating these automated filters.

How to Tailor Your Resume for Specific Roles

To tailor your resume effectively, start by analyzing the job description. Carefully read through it to identify the key skills, experiences, and qualifications the employer seeks. Highlight these requirements and use them as a guide for customizing your resume.

Next, match your skills and experiences to the job requirements. Reflect on your previous roles, projects, and achievements most relevant to the position. This ensures that your resume demonstrates how your background aligns with the job.

Incorporate action words, keywords, and phrases from the job description strategically throughout your resume. Focus on quantifying your achievements wherever possible. Use metrics to demonstrate your impact in previous roles. For example, instead of saying, "Managed a team," say, "Managed a team of 10, increasing productivity by 20% over six months." This provides concrete evidence of your contributions and effectiveness.

Customize each section of your resume to highlight your suitability for the role. This includes the summary, work experience, skills, and education sections. Tailoring each part ensures that your entire resume is cohesive and targeted.

Finally, keep your resume concise and relevant. Remove any information that is not directly relevant to the role. A concise, focused resume is more impactful than a lengthy one filled with unrelated details. This approach ensures that every part of your resume works towards showcasing your fit for the job.

Examples of Tailoring a Resume

Let's consider an example of a generic industry resume and how it can be tailored for specific roles within the information technology industry. Suppose you are in the tech industry with a generic resume focused on software development. We'll tailor this resume for two different roles: a Front-End Developer and a Project Manager in software development.

Generic Software Development Resume:

Summary:

- Experienced software developer with a strong background in various programming languages and software development methodologies. Proven ability to deliver high-quality software solutions on time and within budget.

Work Experience:

- **Sr Software Developer/Project Manager | XYZ Tech Solutions | Jan 2018 – Present**
    - Developed and maintained software applications using Java, Python, and JavaScript.
    - Collaborated with cross-functional teams to gather requirements and implement software solutions.
    - Conducted code reviews and provided mentorship to junior developers.
    - Managed multiple software development projects from inception to completion, ensuring timely delivery and budget adherence.
    - Coordinated with cross-functional teams, including developers, designers, and stakeholders, to define project scope and deliverables.
    - Implemented Agile practices, leading daily stand-ups, sprint planning, and retrospectives.
    - Enhanced team productivity by 20% through process improvements and effective resource management.
- **Junior Software Developer | ABC Technologies | Jun 2015 – Dec 2017**
    - Assisted in developing web applications using HTML, CSS, and JavaScript.
    - Participated in team meetings to discuss project progress and resolve issues.
    - Performed testing and debugging of applications to ensure functionality.

Skills:

- Programming Languages: Java, Python, JavaScript, HTML, CSS
- Software Development: Agile, Scrum, Waterfall
- Tools: Git, JIRA, Jenkins

Education:

- Bachelor of Science in Computer Science | University of Tech | 2015

Tailored Resume for a Front-End Developer Role:

Summary:

- Front-End Developer with 5+ years of experience specializing in creating responsive and visually appealing web applications. Proficient in HTML, CSS, JavaScript, and modern frameworks like React and Angular. Adept at collaborating with design teams to implement UI/UX enhancements.

Work Experience:

- **Front-End Developer | XYZ Tech Solutions | Jan 2018 – Present**
    - Led the development of front-end features for web applications using React and Angular.
    - Collaborated with UX/UI designers to improve user experience, resulting in a 15% increase in user engagement.
    - Implemented responsive design techniques to ensure applications perform well on various devices.
    - Conducted code reviews and guided junior

developers on best practices.

- **Junior Front-End Developer | ABC Technologies | Jun 2015 – Dec 2017**
    - Developed interactive web applications using HTML, CSS, and JavaScript.
    - Worked closely with the design team to translate wireframes into functional web pages.
    - Performed cross-browser testing and debugging to ensure compatibility across different browsers.

Skills:

- Front-End Development: HTML, CSS, JavaScript, React, Angular
- UI/UX Design: Responsive Design, Cross-Browser Compatibility
- Tools: Git, JIRA, Webpack

Education:

- Bachelor of Science in Computer Science | University of Tech | 2015

Tailored Resume for a Project Manager in Software Development Role:

Summary:

- Project Manager with over five years of experience in leading software development projects. Expertise in Agile and Scrum methodologies with a proven track record of delivering projects on time and within budget. Strong leadership and communication skills.

Work Experience:

- **Project Manager | XYZ Tech Solutions | Jan 2018 – Present**
    - Managed multiple software development projects from inception to completion, ensuring timely delivery and budget adherence.
    - Coordinated with cross-functional teams, including developers, designers, and stakeholders, to define project scope and deliverables.
    - Implemented Agile practices, leading daily stand-ups, sprint planning, and retrospectives.
    - Enhanced team productivity by 20% through process improvements and effective resource management.
- **Software Developer | ABC Technologies | Jun 2015 – Dec 2017**
    - Contributed to software development projects using Java, Python, and JavaScript.
    - Assisted in project planning and task allocation in collaboration with the project manager.
    - Participated in code reviews and provided feedback to ensure code quality.

Skills:

- Project Management: Agile, Scrum, Waterfall, Project Planning, Risk Management
- Technical: Java, Python, JavaScript, Software Development
- Tools: JIRA, Confluence, MS Project

Education:

- Bachelor of Science in Computer Science | University of Tech | 2015
- Certified Scrum Master (CSM) | Scrum Alliance | 2018

Final Thoughts

In these examples, the generic resume has been tailored to highlight the specific skills, experiences, and qualifications relevant to the Front-End Developer and Project Manager roles. By focusing on the most pertinent aspects of your background and aligning them with the job requirements, you create a resume that speaks directly to the employer's needs. This targeted approach increases your chances of getting noticed and demonstrates your genuine interest and suitability for the role.

Tailoring your resume is not just about changing a few words but strategically positioning yourself as the ideal candidate for the specific job. By taking the time to customize your resume for each application, you show employers that you are serious about the opportunity and have the skills and experiences they are looking for. Investing in the time to tailor your resume can significantly enhance your job search success and help you secure the desired roles.

FOUR

Working with Recruiters

Whether you are just entering the job market or are a seasoned professional, you will want to have every resource or tool for your hunt at the ready. One often underutilized tool in your arsenal is the professional recruiter or headhunter. These experts can provide otherwise unknown insights on the current state of the job market, access to hidden job opportunities, and invaluable support throughout the job search process.

The Role of Recruiters

Recruiters and headhunters act as intermediaries between job seekers and employers. Their primary function is to match qualified candidates with job openings, often ones not advertised publicly. There are several types of recruiters, including Internal Recruiters, who are Employed by a specific company to fill their job openings; Agency Recruiters, who Work for recruiting agencies and represent multiple clients; and Executive Headhunters, who Specialize in filling high-level executive positions. What you will find in the following guide will apply to all recruiters regardless of their specialization or area of focus.

Why Partner with a Recruiter?

Access to Unadvertised Opportunities

One of the most significant advantages of working with a recruiter is accessing the 'hidden job market.' This market is where many companies may not publicly advertise certain job openings. These unadvertised opportunities, often filtered through a network of trusted recruiters and headhunters, can be the key to finding your dream job.

Benefits of Accessing the Hidden Job Market

Reduced Competition: Since these jobs are not posted on public job boards, the pool of applicants is significantly smaller, increasing your chances of standing out and securing an interview.

Exclusive Opportunities: Recruiters often have exclusive contracts with companies to fill specific positions, meaning you might be considered for roles that are not accessible through any other means.

Faster Hiring Process: Employers using recruiters often seek to fill positions quickly. This can result in a more streamlined hiring process, with quicker interview scheduling and decision-making.

Better Matches: Recruiters strive for more precise matching, with their deep understanding of both the employer's needs and your qualifications. This meticulous approach increases the likelihood of a good fit, reducing the risk of turnover and job dissatisfaction and reassuring job seekers about the potential job fit.

Expertise and Industry Insights

Recruiters possess in-depth knowledge of their respective industries and job markets. Their expertise goes beyond simply knowing which companies are hiring; they have a nuanced understanding of industry trends, salary benchmarks, and the skills in demand.

How Industry Insights Benefit You

Market Trends: Recruiters are aware of emerging trends and shifts within industries. They can advise you on which sectors are growing, which skills are becoming obsolete, and where the highest demand for talent lies.

Salary Information: Knowing the going rate for your role in the current market is crucial for negotiating your salary. Recruiters have access to up-to-date salary data and can help you set realistic expectations or negotiate higher pay based on your skills and experience.

Skill Development: Recruiters can identify gaps in your skill set and suggest areas for improvement or additional training. This advice can make you more competitive and attractive to potential employers.

Company Culture and Fit: Beyond job descriptions, recruiters have insights into company cultures and work environments. They can help ensure that you find a role that matches your skills and one where you will thrive and be satisfied.

Streamlined Job Search Process

Job hunting can be time-consuming and overwhelming. Recruiters can streamline the process by handling time-consuming tasks and using their expertise to facilitate a more efficient search.

How Recruiters Streamline the Job Search

Resume Matching: Recruiters use their knowledge of job descriptions and employers to match their resumes with appropriate job openings, saving them time and effort in tailoring applications.

Interview Arrangements: Recruiters schedule interviews and provide logistical support, freeing you from the administrative burden. They often coordinate between you and the employer, ensuring the process moves smoothly.

Feedback Loop: After each interview, recruiters gather feedback from the employer and share it with you. This constructive feedback helps you improve your interview performance and understand employers' needs.

Negotiation Assistance: Recruiters can act as intermediaries during salary and benefit negotiations, leveraging their knowledge and experience to secure the best possible terms for you.

Personalized Support and Feedback

A good recruiter provides personalized support throughout the job search process. They offer guidance and feedback tailored to your unique situation and goals.

Components of Personalized Support

Resume Refinement: Recruiters can help you craft a resume highlighting your strengths and aligning with the job market's demands. They can offer tips on formatting, keyword usage, and emphasizing relevant experiences.

Interview Preparation: Recruiters provide valuable insights into the interview process, including common questions, employer expectations, and tips for presenting yourself effectively. They might conduct mock interviews to help you practice and gain confidence.

Constructive Feedback: Recruiters provide detailed feedback on your performance after each interview. They can pinpoint areas for improvement and offer specific advice on better articulating your skills and experiences.

Career Coaching: Beyond immediate job search needs, recruiters often offer long-term career coaching. They can help you map out your career path, set achievable goals, and identify opportunities for professional growth.

Finding the Right Recruiter

Finding the right recruiter can significantly impact your job search success. A good recruiter not only understands your career goals but also has the right industry connections and expertise to help you achieve them. Here's a detailed guide on how to find the right recruiter for your needs.

Research and Recommendations

Conduct Thorough Research

Start by identifying recruiters who specialize in your industry or job function. Specialized recruiters have a deeper understanding of the specific skills, qualifications, and experiences required for roles in your field.

Industry-Specific Recruiters: Look for recruiters who focus on your industry, whether technology, finance, healthcare, marketing, or any other sector. They will be more knowledgeable about the market trends and opportunities within that industry.

Function-Specific Recruiters: If your job role is specialized, such as data science, legal counsel, or executive leadership, find recruiters who specialize in those functions.

Seek Recommendations

Personal recommendations can be invaluable in finding a trustworthy recruiter.

Colleagues and Professional Contacts: Ask your colleagues, mentors, or industry peers if they have worked with any recruiters they would recommend.

Industry Groups and Associations: Join industry-specific groups and associations online and offline. These communities often have forums or networking events where you can gather recommendations.

Online Reviews and LinkedIn: Check online reviews and ratings on platforms like Glassdoor or Indeed. Use LinkedIn to search for recruiters in your field and read their profiles and recommendations from other professionals.

Assess Their Network and Experience

A recruiter's network and experience are critical indicators of their ability to help you find the right job.

Evaluate Their Network

A well-connected recruiter has established relationships with hiring managers and decision-makers across various companies. This network can open doors to exclusive job opportunities not advertised publicly.

Client Base: Inquire about the companies they typically work with. Are these companies aligned with your career goals and values?

Industry Presence: Check if the recruiter is active in industry events, conferences, and seminars. Active participation indicates a strong network and up-to-date knowledge of industry trends.

Review Their Experience

Experience is another crucial factor. An experienced recruiter understands the nuances of the job market and can provide valuable guidance throughout your job search.

Track Record: Ask about their success rate in placing candidates in similar roles. A high success rate indicates that the recruiter has a good understanding of what employers in your field are looking for.

Longevity: Consider how long the recruiter has been in the business. A recruiter with a long-standing career will likely have a more extensive network and a better reputation.

Initial Consultation

Once you have shortlisted potential recruiters, arrange an initial consultation to evaluate their suitability.

Gauge Their Expertise

Use the initial meeting to assess the recruiter's knowledge and expertise.

Understanding Your Field: Discuss your career goals and ask questions about the industry and job market. A knowledgeable recruiter can provide insightful answers and offer relevant advice.

Success Stories: Ask for examples of how they have successfully placed candidates in positions similar to what you seek. This will give you an idea of their capability and effectiveness.

Understand Their Approach

When choosing a recruiter, it's essential to understand how they plan to work with you and market you to potential employers. A recruiter's approach can significantly impact your job search experience and outcomes. Here's a deeper look into what you should ask and expect from your recruiter's process, communication style, and client profiles.

Process Explanation

Understanding the recruiter's process for finding and submitting candidates is crucial. This includes how they match candidates to job openings, prepare them for interviews, and handle negotiations.

Matching Candidates to Job Openings

Initial Assessment: Ask how the recruiter assesses your skills, experience, and career goals. Do they use a standardized form, a detailed interview, or a combination?

Job Matching Criteria: Understand their criteria to match you with potential job openings. Do they prioritize skill fit, cultural fit, or both?

Submission Process: Inquire about the process of submitting your resume to employers. Will they inform you before sending your application, or do they submit it based on their judgment?

Interview Preparation

Preparation Materials: Ask if they provide resources or materials to help you prepare for interviews, such as potential questions, company background, and tips for success.

Mock Interviews: Find out if they offer mock interviews or coaching sessions to help you practice and improve your interview skills.

Feedback Loop: Understand how they gather and share feedback from interviews. This feedback can be crucial for improving your performance in future interviews.

Handling Negotiations

Salary Negotiation: Ask about their role in salary negotiations. Will they negotiate on your behalf, provide guidance to negotiate directly, or keep you out of the loop after learning your desired salary?

Benefit Discussions: Find out if they help negotiate other aspects of the job offer, such as benefits, working conditions, and job responsibilities.

Counteroffers: Understand their approach to handling counteroffers. Will they assist you in evaluating and responding to counteroffers from your current or prospective employer?

Communication Style

Clear and regular communication is vital for a successful recruiter-candidate relationship. Clarify how often and through what channels they will communicate with you.

Frequency of Communication

Establish expectations between yourself and the recruiter. Remember, every recruiter is different, and each will have their own methods in how they work.

Regular Updates: Ask how often you can expect updates on your job search status, new job openings, and employer feedback.

Availability: Find out if they are available for questions and support throughout the week or if they have specific office hours.

Channels of Communication

Preferred Methods: Understand their preferred communication methods, such as email, phone calls, text messages, or video calls.

Responsiveness: Ask about their typical response time to emails or calls. Quick responses can be crucial during time-sensitive negotiations or interview preparations.

Client Profiles

Understanding a recruiter's typical clients can help determine if their client base aligns with your career aspirations.

Industry Focus

Sector Specialization: Ask if they specialize in specific industries or sectors. A recruiter with expertise in your industry is more likely to have relevant job opportunities.

Company Types: Inquire about the companies they usually work with, such as startups, mid-sized firms, or large corporations.

Job Levels

Position Levels: Understand the levels of positions they typically fill, whether it's entry-level, mid-level, or executive roles.

Career Progression: Ask if they have experience placing candidates in roles that offer growth and advancement opportunities aligned with your career goals.

Staff Augmentation vs Direct Hire Recruiters

Understanding the difference between a staff augmentation recruiter and a placement recruiter is essential for aligning your job search strategy with the right type of recruiter.

Staff Augmentation Recruiter

A staff augmentation recruiter focuses on providing temporary or contract workers to companies. They help businesses fill short-term needs for specific projects or peak demand periods.

Contract and Temporary Roles: These recruiters specialize in filling contract and temporary positions rather than permanent roles.

Project-Based Hiring: Companies often use staff augmentation recruiters for specific projects requiring specialized skills.

Flexibility: Candidates working with these recruiters typically have the flexibility to work on various projects for different companies over time.

Ongoing Support: Staff augmentation recruiters often maintain an ongoing relationship with their contractors, placing them in multiple short-term roles as they become available.

Direct Hire Recruiter

A placement recruiter, also known as a direct-hire or permanent placement recruiter, focuses on finding candidates for permanent, full-time positions within a company.

Permanent Roles: These recruiters specialize in filling long-term, permanent positions.

Full-Time Employment: Candidates are placed directly with the hiring company as full-time employees, usually with a benefits package.

Career Development: Placement recruiters often focus on matching candidates with roles that align with their long-term career goals.

Employer-Employee Fit: They emphasize finding a good cultural and organizational fit between the candidate and the employer to ensure long-term success.

Working Effectively with Your Recruiter

Partnering with a recruiter can significantly enhance your job search but requires a proactive and cooperative approach.

Open, Honest Communication

Establishing open and honest communication is crucial for a successful partnership with your recruiter.

Articulate Your Career Goals and Preferences

Define Your Objectives: Clearly state your short-term and long-term career goals. Whether you are looking for a specific role, industry, or company size, ensure your recruiter understands your objectives.

List Your Preferences: Include preferences such as job location, salary expectations, company culture, and work-life balance. Identify the top three things that are most important to you in your next position.

Discuss Constraints: Be upfront about any constraints, such as relocation limitations, family commitments, or other personal considerations that may affect your job search.

Regular Updates

Availability Changes: Inform your recruiter about any changes in your availability, such as periods when you might not be able to attend interviews or new time frames for starting a job.

Preference Adjustments: If your career goals or preferences change, update your recruiter promptly. This ensures they continue to search for opportunities that align with your evolving needs.

Be Honest and Transparent

Honesty is fundamental in building a trust-based relationship with your recruiter.

Accurate Information

Skills and Experience: Provide a truthful account of your skills, experience, and job history. This helps the recruiter find the best matches for your qualifications.

Employment Gaps: Discuss these openly if you have gaps in your employment history or other potential red flags. A good recruiter can help you frame these gaps positively and address employers' concerns.

Discuss Potential Issues

Failed Background Checks: Transparency in addressing any concerns about your background is important. A failed background check will negatively impact you by raising concerns about your reliability and trustworthiness, potentially leading to the interview being canceled or the job offer being rescinded.

Work Preferences: Be transparent about what you seek in a job, including the tasks and responsibilities you prefer or wish to avoid.

Feedback and Concerns: If you have any concerns about job opportunities or the recruitment process, communicate them to your recruiter. This will allow them to address the issues and refine their search accordingly.

Stay Proactive

While recruiters play a pivotal role in your job search, you must also remain actively involved in the process.

Respect Their Time and Efforts

Recruiters manage multiple candidates and clients, so respecting their time and efforts is essential.

Prompt Responses

Timely Communication: Respond promptly to emails, calls, and messages from your recruiter. Delayed responses can slow down the job search process.

Document Submission: Provide requested documents, such as your resume, cover letters, and references, in a timely manner.

Punctuality

Interview Attendance: Attend scheduled interviews punctually. If you need to reschedule, inform your recruiter as soon as possible.

Meeting Deadlines: Adhere to deadlines set by your recruiter for tasks like completing applications or preparing for interviews.

Provide Feedback

Providing feedback after each interview helps your recruiter fine-tune their search and offer better guidance.

Interview Performance

What Went Well: Share what you felt went well during the interview. This helps your recruiter understand your strengths.

Areas of Concern: Highlight areas where you felt unsure or encountered difficulties. This feedback can help your recruiter provide targeted advice for future interviews.

Interest Level

Job Suitability: Based on your interview experience, let your recruiter know you are interested in the position. If the role does not seem like a good fit, explain why.

Employer Impressions: Provide your impressions of the employer and the work environment. This information can help your recruiter refine their search to match your preferences better.

Limit the Number of Recruiters You Work With

When navigating the job market, you may be tempted to work with multiple recruiters to maximize your exposure to job opportunities. However, this strategy will likely backfire, especially when working with more than three simultaneously. Limiting the number of recruiters you work with is crucial, enabling you to maintain control over your job search, ensure a cohesive and focused strategy, and preserve your professional reputation.

Ensuring a Cohesive Job Search Strategy

Working with a limited number of recruiters helps maintain a cohesive and strategic approach to your job search.

Consistent Messaging

Unified Representation: With fewer recruiters, you can ensure that your resume and professional profile are presented consistently to potential employers.

Avoiding Confusion: Different recruiters might emphasize different aspects of your experience and skills, leading to mixed messages that could confuse employers.

Focused Search

Targeted Opportunities: A smaller group of recruiters can better understand your career goals and preferences, allowing for a more targeted and effective job search.

Quality Over Quantity: Instead of being submitted for a wide range of positions that may not align with your goals, you can focus on high-quality opportunities that better fit your career path.

Maintaining Control Over Your Job Search

Limiting the number of recruiters you work with allows you to control your job search process better.

Avoiding Overlap

Duplicate Submissions: Multiple recruiters submitting your resume to the same company can create confusion and even harm your chances of being considered for a position.

Managing Conflicts: It becomes easier to manage and avoid conflicts between recruiters with competing interests or different relationships with potential employers.

Streamlined Communication

Centralized Updates: With fewer recruiters, you can more effectively keep track of your applications and receive regular updates on your job search status.

Efficient Feedback Loop: You can more easily manage feedback from interviews and recruiters, allowing you to make necessary adjustments to your job search strategy.

Preserving Professional Reputation

Your professional reputation is paramount, and working with a limited number of recruiters helps maintain a positive image in the job market.

Employer Perception

Professionalism: Employers may perceive you as more professional and serious about your job search if you are not being represented by numerous recruiters simultaneously.

Avoiding Red Flags: Being represented by too many recruiters can raise red flags for employers, who might question your ability to secure a job independently or view you as less desirable.

Relationship Building

Stronger Relationships: Building solid relationships with a few recruiters can lead to more personalized and dedicated support.

Trust and Loyalty: Recruiters are more likely to invest time and effort in candidates who show loyalty and trust in their services.

How to Effectively Limit Your Recruiter Engagements

To effectively limit the number of recruiters you work with, consider the following strategies:

Select Specialization

Choose recruiters who specialize in your industry or job function. Specialized recruiters have a deeper understanding of the market and can provide more relevant opportunities.

Industry Experts: Recruiters with a niche focus in your industry are likelier to have strong relationships with key employers and understand the specific skills and qualifications needed.

Function Experts: Recruiters specializing in your job function (e.g., marketing, finance, IT) can offer tailored opportunities that align with your expertise.

Vet Recruiters Thoroughly

Take the time to vet recruiters before deciding to work with them.

Track Record: Look for recruiters with a proven track record of placing candidates in roles similar to what you are seeking.

Reputation: Check reviews, testimonials, and recommendations from other candidates to gauge the recruiter's reputation and effectiveness.

Initial Consultation: To understand their approach, communication style, and how they plan to represent you in the job market.

Set Clear Expectations

Establish clear expectations and boundaries with your chosen recruiters.

Preferred Roles: Communicate the types of roles and companies you are interested in.

Submission Protocol: Agree on a protocol for submitting your resume to potential employers to avoid duplicate submissions.

Regular Updates: Ensure that there is a plan for regular updates and feedback throughout the job search process.

Final Thoughts

Finding and partnering with a good recruiter or headhunter can significantly enhance your job search efforts. You can access hidden opportunities and receive personalized support by tapping into their expertise, industry insights, and networks. Conduct thorough research, establish clear communication, and maintain a proactive and respectful approach. With the right recruiter, you can navigate the job market more effectively and achieve your career goals.

FIVE

Interview Styles and How to Handle Them

Different interview styles exist, each with a specific purpose. By understanding these styles and how to approach them, job seekers can significantly enhance their chances of success. Here, we will explore the ten most common interview styles and provide strategies to effectively navigate each one, empowering you to take control of your interview experience.

Each interview style requires a tailored approach to effectively showcase your strengths and potential. You will be armed with the best practices for preparing for and succeeding in these interview formats, equipping you with the tools to make a lasting impression and secure your desired roles.

Interview Styles

Structured Interviews:

This style involves a standardized set of questions asked of every candidate, focusing on skills and experiences relevant to the job. It ensures fairness and consistency, making it easier to compare candidates, and is best suited for large organizations and roles with clearly defined requirements.

Unstructured Interviews:

This is a more casual and conversational interview style where the interviewer has a general idea of topics to cover but does not follow a strict script. It allows for a more natural conversation and can provide deeper insights into the candidate's personality and cultural fit, making it ideal for creative roles and positions where personality and fit are critical.

Behavioral Interviews:

This interview style focuses on how candidates have handled past situations and challenges, with questions typically starting with "Tell me about a time when..." and requiring specific examples. It provides insight into how candidates apply their skills and experience in real-world situations, making it best suited for positions requiring specific competencies and past experience.

Situational Interviews:

In this interview style, candidates are presented with hypothetical situations related to the job and asked how they would handle them. It tests problem-solving skills and the ability to think independently, making it best suited for roles involving frequent decision-making or problem-solving.

Panel Interviews:

This type of interview involves multiple interviewers questioning a single candidate, with each interviewer focusing on different aspects of the candidate's qualifications. It provides multiple perspectives on the candidate and can be more efficient than multiple one-on-one interviews, making it ideal for high-stakes positions and senior roles.

Group Interviews:

In a group interview setting, multiple candidates are interviewed together, often engaging in discussions or problem-solving sessions. This format allows interviewers to observe how candidates interact with others, assessing their teamwork and leadership skills in real time. It is particularly beneficial for roles that demand strong interpersonal skills, such as sales or customer service positions.

Technical Interviews:

Technical interviews focus on assessing candidates' technical skills and knowledge through tasks such as problem-solving exercises, coding tests, or technical questions. This format directly evaluates the candidate's ability to perform job-specific tasks, making it particularly suitable for IT, engineering, and other technical roles where specialized expertise is crucial.

Case Interviews:

Case interviews present candidates with a business problem and require them to propose a solution, commonly used in consulting and finance industries. This format tests candidates' analytical and problem-solving abilities within a realistic business context, making it ideal for roles in consulting, finance, and strategic management where practical problem-solving skills are essential.

Telephonic/Video Interviews

Remote interviews are conducted via phone or video conferencing tools, which are convenient and cost-effective, particularly for preliminary screenings or when interviewing long-distance candidates. This format is ideal for initial assessments before in-person meetings and is well-suited for remote roles or requires candidates to work from a distance.

Competency-Based Interviews:

The competency-based interview section evaluates candidates' skills and competencies essential for the role, such as teamwork, leadership, and communication. Questions are designed to probe specific competencies to ensure candidates possess the required abilities and behaviors for the position. This approach is most effective for roles with clearly defined competency requirements, allowing interviewers to assess candidates comprehensively based on their demonstrated capabilities.

Each interview style has its strengths and is best suited for different types of roles and organizational needs. Employers often use a combination of these styles to comprehensively understand a candidate's suitability for a position.

How to approach most used interview styles

Unstructured Interviews

Unstructured interviews are characterized by their casual and conversational nature, where interviewers often allow the discussion to flow naturally without adhering to a strict script. To prepare effectively, it's essential to research the company's culture, values, and recent developments. Familiarize yourself thoroughly with your resume, anticipating questions about your experiences and achievements. Prepare anecdotes that showcase your skills and accomplishments to illustrate your suitability for the role. If you encounter unexpected questions, take a moment to gather your thoughts and respond thoughtfully. Remember, the interviewer is interested in your thought process and how you handle unexpected situations.

Aim to engage in a two-way conversation with the interviewer during the interview, demonstrating genuine interest and enthusiasm. Be adaptable and flexible, as the discussion may cover a wide range of topics beyond the typical interview questions. Show your curiosity and engagement by asking thoughtful questions that reflect your interest in the company and the role. If you find yourself feeling nervous or anxious, take a deep breath and remind yourself of your preparation and qualifications. Remember, the interview is also an opportunity for you to assess if the company and role are a good fit for you.

After the interview, send a thank-you note to express appreciation for the opportunity and reaffirm your interest in the position. Reflect on the interview experience, considering what went well and areas for improvement to enhance your performance in future interviews. This approach ensures you make a positive impression and effectively communicate your qualifications and enthusiasm for the role.

Behavioral Interviews

Behavioral interviews center on past behavior as a predictor of future performance, typically beginning with questions like "Tell me about a time when..." To prepare effectively, identify key competencies outlined in the job description to understand the specific skills and behaviors the employer seeks. Utilize the STAR Method (Situation, Task, Action, Result) to structure your responses, ensuring clarity and coherence in illustrating your capabilities. Prepare specific examples from your professional experiences demonstrating these competencies to provide concrete evidence of your qualifications.

During the interview, focus on being specific and detailed when sharing examples, highlighting your role and contributions in each situation. Maintain honesty and authenticity throughout, avoiding the temptation to embellish or exaggerate your experiences. Emphasize the positive outcomes and results achieved through your actions to underscore your effectiveness in applying skills and solving problems.

After the interview, reinforce key points discussed by mentioning critical examples in your thank-you note to reaffirm your suitability for the role. Stay prepared by reflecting on the interview questions and experiences to refine your responses and readiness for future behavioral interviews continuously. This structured approach ensures you effectively demonstrate your capabilities and align with the employer's expectations during the hiring process.

Situational Interviews

Situational interviews involve presenting hypothetical scenarios relevant to the job and assessing how candidates would respond. To prepare effectively, research common challenges within the industry or specific role. Develop a problem-solving framework that includes identifying the issue, analyzing potential solutions, and proposing a course of action—practice by considering various scenarios and strategizing how you would approach each one.

During the interview, articulate your thought process clearly by thinking aloud and demonstrating your reasoning behind each decision. Maintaining a structured approach when addressing the scenario ensures your response follows a logical sequence. Explore different angles to the problem to showcase your ability to consider multiple perspectives, highlighting your critical thinking skills and adaptability.

After the interview, in your thank-you note, briefly summarize how you handled a key scenario discussed during the interview to reinforce your suitability for the role. Take time to review your performance, reflecting on your responses and areas for improvement to enhance your readiness for future situational interviews. This proactive approach helps you effectively demonstrate your problem-solving abilities and align with the employer's expectations throughout the hiring process.

Panel Interviews

Panel interviews involve multiple interviewers directing questions at a single candidate, each focusing on different aspects of the candidate's qualifications. If you can find out who the panel members are before the interview, then it is often helpful to research them to understand their organizational roles and perspectives. Anticipate diverse questions about your experience and skills and how they align with the job requirements. Practice for the dynamic of a panel interview by simulating scenarios where multiple individuals ask questions simultaneously or consecutively.

During the interview, demonstrate professionalism by addressing each interviewer individually, maintaining eye contact, and thoughtfully engaging with their questions. Stay composed and confident, even when faced with rapid-fire questioning, ensuring your responses are concise yet comprehensive to accommodate all panel members' inquiries. Manage your time effectively to provide thorough answers while allowing each interviewer an opportunity to participate actively.

After the interview, send personalized thank-you notes to each panel member to express gratitude for their time and insights. In your notes, recap specific points or questions discussed with each interviewer to reinforce your suitability for the role and demonstrate your attentiveness during the interview process. This approach shows appreciation and reaffirms your interest and alignment with the organization's expectations, enhancing your chances of making a positive impression.

Case Interviews

Case interviews involve presenting candidates with a business problem to assess their problem-solving abilities through analysis and recommendation. To prepare effectively, start by studying common case interview frameworks such as SWOT analysis, Porter's Five Forces, and the 4Ps (Product, Price, Place, Promotion). Practice solving cases independently or with a partner to familiarize yourself with different scenarios and refine your approach.

Enhance your analytical skills by working on data analysis and logical reasoning techniques. During the interview, clarify the problem statement before diving into your analysis. Structure your response, organize your approach, and communicate it effectively to the interviewer. Incorporate relevant data and quantitative analysis to support your solution, demonstrating your ability to use data effectively in decision-making.

Throughout the interview, think aloud to share your analytical thought process with the interviewer, illustrating how you approach and solve complex problems. Afterward, summarize your proposed solution in a thank-you note, briefly restating the problem and outlining your recommended approach. Reflect on any feedback received during the interview to identify areas for improvement in your case-solving skills, ensuring continuous growth and readiness for future case interviews. This proactive approach helps you effectively showcase your analytical abilities and strategic thinking to potential employers.

Telephonic/Video Interviews

Remote interviews are conducted as a preliminary screening tool, offering convenience for both candidates and employers. To prepare effectively, ensure your technology setup, whether phone or video conferencing, is in good working order and that you have a stable internet connection. Select a quiet and distraction-free location for the interview, and approach your preparation with the same diligence as you would for an in-person interview—dress professionally and have your resume and notes readily accessible.

During the interview, prioritize punctuality by joining the call on time or a few minutes early. Speak clearly and confidently to ensure your communication is articulate and easy to understand. Maintain a high level of professionalism throughout the remote interview, treating it with the seriousness and respect typically given to face-to-face meetings.

After the interview, send a thank-you email to express appreciation for the opportunity and reaffirm your interest in the position. Take time to reflect on the experience, noting any technical issues or areas where you can improve to better prepare for future remote interviews. This approach demonstrates your professionalism and proactive attitude, leaving a positive impression on potential employers.

Final Thoughts

Let's face it—job hunting is competitive. Mastering various interview styles is valuable for standing out and securing your desired positions. Understanding the purpose and structure of each interview type allows you to tailor your preparation and approach accordingly, enhancing your performance and increasing your chances of success.

SIX

Common Interview Questions

In any job interview, preparation is key to presenting yourself as the best candidate to the potential employer. Understanding and effectively answering common interview questions can significantly enhance your chances of success. Here, we explore the top 15 common interview questions, regardless of the industry, along with strategies and examples to help you formulate strong responses.

Tell me about yourself.

Objective: This question allows you to introduce yourself and highlight your relevant experiences and skills.

Strategy: Keep your response concise and focused on your professional background. Structure your answer from your current role or education to how it aligns with the job you're applying for.

Example: "I graduated with a degree in marketing and have spent the last five years working for digital marketing agencies. My strengths lie in social media strategy and content creation, which I believe align well with the innovative approach your company is known for."

Why do you want to work here?

Objective: Interviewers use this question to gauge your interest in the company and the role.

Strategy: Research the company beforehand to understand its mission, values, and recent achievements. Tailor your response to show how your skills and career goals align with the company's objectives.

Example: "I've been following your company's growth in sustainable technology, and I'm particularly drawn to your commitment to reducing carbon emissions. I believe my background in renewable energy project management would be a valuable addition to your team."

What are your strengths?

Objective: This question allows you to showcase your key skills and attributes relevant to the job.

Strategy: Select strengths that directly relate to the position and provide examples or achievements to back them up.

Example: "My organizational skills are one of my strongest assets. In my previous role as an office manager, I implemented a new filing system that reduced retrieval time by 30%, improving overall office efficiency."

What are your weaknesses?

Objective: Interviewers ask this to assess your self-awareness and ability to improve.

Strategy: Be honest but focus on a weakness that is not crucial to the job or one that you're actively working to improve.

Example: "I used to struggle with public speaking, but I've been taking courses and volunteering for presentations to build my confidence, and I've seen significant improvement."

Can you describe a challenging situation and how you dealt with it?

Objective: This question tests your problem-solving and resilience skills.

Strategy: Structure your answer using the STAR method (Situation, Task, Action, Result), emphasizing how you overcame obstacles and achieved a positive outcome.

Example: "In my previous role, we faced a sudden budget cut that threatened a key project. I collaborated with stakeholders to prioritize tasks, reallocate resources, and successfully complete the project within the revised budget."

Why are you leaving your current job (or why did you leave your last job)?

Objective: Employers want to understand your reasons for job changes and ensure you're leaving on good terms.

Strategy: Be honest but focus on seeking new challenges or opportunities for growth that align with the position you're applying for.

Example: "I'm looking for a role that offers more opportunities to lead projects independently and contribute to strategic decision-making, which I believe aligns with the opportunities at your company."

Where do you see yourself in five years?

Objective: This question helps interviewers gauge your career ambitions and see if they align with the company's trajectory.

Strategy: Express your desire for growth and learning within the company while emphasizing your commitment to contributing effectively.

Example: "In five years, I see myself as a senior project manager, leveraging my expertise to drive impactful projects and mentoring junior team members."

How do you handle stress and pressure?

Objective: Interviewers ask this to assess your ability to perform under challenging conditions.

Strategy: Provide specific examples of how you stay organized and maintain focus during stressful times.

Example: "I prioritize tasks based on deadlines and importance and regularly communicate with my team to ensure we're aligned on goals. Taking short breaks for mindfulness exercises also helps me stay focused and productive."

Describe a time when you worked as part of a team.

Objective: This question assesses your teamwork and collaboration skills.

Strategy: Highlight your role within the team, how you contributed to achieving team goals, and any challenges you successfully navigated.

Example: "I led a cross-functional team to launch a new product, coordinating efforts between marketing, sales, and product development. By fostering open communication and setting clear milestones, we exceeded our sales targets by 20%."

Why should we hire you?

Objective: This is your opportunity to differentiate yourself and demonstrate why you're the best fit for the job.

Strategy: Summarize your unique qualifications, experiences, and passion for the role, emphasizing how you can bring value to the company.

Example: "With my background in data analysis and proven track record of improving operational efficiency, I'm confident that I can help streamline your processes and contribute to your company's growth objectives."

Tell me about a time you demonstrated leadership skills.

Objective: This question assesses your ability to lead and influence others.

Strategy: Choose an example where you took initiative, motivated others, and achieved a significant outcome.

Example: "As a team leader on a complex IT project, I delegated tasks based on team members' strengths, provided mentorship, and facilitated weekly progress meetings. We completed the project ahead of schedule and received positive feedback from stakeholders."

Can you provide an example of a project you successfully managed?

Objective: Interviewers ask this to evaluate your project management skills and ability to deliver results.

Strategy: Describe the project scope, your role, challenges faced, actions taken, and measurable outcomes achieved.

Example: "I managed a website redesign project, overseeing a team of designers and developers. By implementing Agile methodologies and conducting regular client feedback sessions, we launched the new site on time, resulting in a 40% increase in user engagement."

How do you prioritize your work?

Objective: Employers want to know how you manage multiple tasks and deadlines effectively.

Strategy: Explain your prioritization method, whether it's based on deadlines, importance, or strategic goals.

Example: "I use a combination of time management tools and weekly planning sessions to prioritize tasks. I focus on high-impact activities first while ensuring I meet project deadlines and client expectations."

What do you know about our company?

Objective: This question tests your knowledge of the company and your interest in the role.

Strategy: Research the company's history, products or services, recent news, and industry reputation. Tailor your answer to reflect your understanding and enthusiasm.

Example: "I admire your company's commitment to sustainability, evidenced by your recent initiatives to reduce carbon emissions across your supply chain. Your innovative approach to renewable energy solutions aligns perfectly with my career aspirations."

Do you have any questions for us?

Objective: Asking questions demonstrates your interest in the role and company while allowing you to gather more information to assess if it's the right fit for you.

Strategy: Prepare thoughtful questions about the team dynamics, company culture, opportunities for growth, or the next steps in the hiring process.

Example: "Could you tell me more about the team dynamics within the department? How does this role contribute to the company's long-term goals?"

Handling Personal or Inappropriate Questions During an Interview

Encountering personal or inappropriate questions during an interview can be uncomfortable and challenging. It's essential to handle these situations professionally and tactfully. First and foremost, remember that you have the right to maintain your privacy. If a question feels too personal or irrelevant to the job, you can diplomatically steer the conversation back to your qualifications and experiences. For example, if asked about your marital status or family plans, you might respond with, "I'm very focused on my career and excited about the professional opportunities this role offers." This redirects the conversation without directly addressing the personal question.

If the question seems unintentionally inappropriate, gently reframe it in a way that relates to the job. For instance, if asked about your age, you could say, "I bring a wealth of experience and energy to my work, and I am excited to contribute my skills to this position." This approach helps you stay positive and keeps the discussion relevant to your professional capabilities.

In cases where a question crosses a clear boundary or feels discriminatory, it's crucial to stay calm and professional. You might respond by saying, "I believe that my skills and experience are the most relevant factors for this role. Could we discuss how my background aligns with the job requirements?" This asserts your professional boundaries and reinforces the focus on your qualifications.

If inappropriate questions persist, it might be a red flag about the company's culture. Trust your instincts and consider whether this environment would make you feel comfortable working. After the interview, you can also choose to report such experiences to the company's HR department or seek guidance from professional organizations that advocate for fair hiring practices.

Final Thoughts

Understanding and effectively answering common interview questions can significantly enhance your chances of success. This chapter explored the top 15 common interview questions, regardless of the industry, along with strategies and examples to help you formulate strong responses.

By understanding the objectives behind these typical interview questions and crafting well-prepared responses, you can showcase your qualifications effectively and leave a lasting impression on your interviewers. Practice these strategies with examples relevant to your experiences to build confidence and readiness for any interview, regardless of the industry.

The ability to navigate personal or inappropriate questions tactfully is also crucial. Remember that you always have the right to maintain privacy and steer the conversation back to your qualifications and experiences. Handling such questions professionally reflects your composure and demonstrates your focus and relevance to the job.

Ultimately, mastering these common interview questions and knowing how to handle challenging ones will equip you with the confidence and skills needed to succeed. As you prepare for your next opportunity, use these insights to tailor your responses, showcase your unique strengths, and align your career goals with the company's mission and values. With thorough preparation and a positive mindset, you can turn any interview into a stepping stone towards your professional growth and success.

SEVEN

The Negotiation

In the intricate dance of job hunting, negotiating a salary or contract stands as one of the most crucial and often anxiety-inducing steps. This process sets the foundation for your financial future and defines your value and worth in the workplace. Yet, with careful preparation and strategic thinking, you can master this art to secure a favorable outcome.

The Importance of Salary Negotiation

Salary negotiation is a critical aspect of the job search process because it directly affects income, a primary motivator for most people in their careers. It sets the baseline for future raises and bonuses, influences your lifestyle, and determines your ability to meet financial goals, whether they be buying a home, saving for retirement, or paying off student loans.

Moreover, how you negotiate your salary can also reflect your professional skills and confidence. Employers often expect candidates to negotiate and view those who do as more assertive and aware of their value. This can set a positive tone for your tenure with the company, demonstrating that you are capable and confident in your abilities.

Understanding Your Worth and Total Compensation

The first step in any successful negotiation is understanding your worth. This means conducting thorough research on industry standards, average salaries for your role in your geographical area, and the specific company's pay scale. Websites like Glassdoor, Payscale, and LinkedIn Salary Insights can provide valuable data. Additionally, networking with professionals and recruiters in your field can give you insider information that might not be available online.

However, understanding your worth goes beyond just numbers. It encompasses your skills, experience, education, and the unique value you bring to the table. Reflect on your career achievements and how they align with the job you're applying for. Are you bringing in a rare skill set? Have you consistently delivered exceptional results? Your negotiation should emphasize these points to justify your asking price.

It's also crucial to look at the total compensation package, not just the base salary. Total compensation includes bonuses, stock options, health benefits, retirement contributions, vacation time, and other perks. Sometimes, a slightly lower base salary might be offset by generous benefits or substantial bonuses. Understanding and evaluating the complete package will give you a clearer picture of the actual value of the offer.

The Power of an 'Unspoken' Range

Having an 'unspoken' range in mind—your ideal salary and the minimum you're willing to accept—can provide a strong foundation for your negotiation. Your ideal salary should be based on your research and reflect what you believe your skills and experience are worth. Your minimum acceptable salary is your bottom line, below which you are not willing to go.

This unspoken range gives you flexibility during negotiations. When you enter a discussion with a clear understanding of your range, you can navigate offers and counteroffers more effectively. For example, if the employer's offer is below your ideal but within your acceptable range, you can negotiate confidently, knowing that you have a clear threshold.

Timing and Strategy

Timing can significantly impact the outcome of your negotiation. The best time to discuss salary is after you've been offered the job but before you've accepted it. At this stage, the employer has already decided that you are the right fit for the position, giving you more leverage.

During the interview process, if the topic of salary comes up prematurely, it's best to deflect it gently. You might say something like, "I'd love to discuss compensation, but first, I'd like to ensure I'm the right fit for the team and the company. Can we revisit this after we've discussed the role in more detail?" This shows that you are focused on the value you can bring and not just the paycheck.

The Power of Silence and Listening

One of the most underrated skills in negotiation is the power of silence. After you've stated your desired salary, resist the urge to fill the silence. This can be uncomfortable, but it places the ball in the employer's court and pressures them to respond.

Listening is equally important. Pay attention to the employer's reactions and responses. They might provide insights into what they value most, which you can then use to bolster your case. If they express concerns about budget constraints, you can negotiate for non-monetary benefits such as additional vacation days, flexible working hours, or professional development opportunities.

Be Prepared for Counteroffers

Employers will often come back with a counteroffer. This is a normal part of the negotiation process and should not be taken as a rejection. Evaluate the counteroffer carefully. Does it meet your minimum requirements? Are there other benefits that make up for a lower salary?

If the counteroffer is significantly lower than your expectations, it's okay to respectfully decline and reiterate your worth. You could say, "I appreciate the offer. However, based on my experience and the industry standards, I was hoping for something closer to [your desired salary]. Is there any flexibility?"

Practice Makes Perfect

Negotiation is a skill that improves with practice. Role-playing with a trusted friend, mentor, or career coach can help you build confidence and anticipate potential responses. Rehearse your key points, but also practice being flexible and thinking on your feet.

It's also helpful to document your negotiation experiences. What strategies worked? What didn't? Learning from each experience will make you a more adept negotiator in the future.

Common Mistakes in Salary Negotiation

There are several common mistakes to avoid in salary negotiations. First, never accept the first offer immediately. Even if it seems generous, it's often a starting point for further negotiation. Take the time to evaluate it and compare it to your researched salary range.

Avoid being overly aggressive or confrontational. This can create a negative impression and damage the relationship before it even begins. Instead, aim for a collaborative approach, where both parties feel they are working towards a common goal.

Another mistake is focusing solely on salary and ignoring other aspects of the compensation package. Benefits, work-life balance, and career growth opportunities can be just as important as salary. Evaluate the entire package to make an informed decision.

Leveraging Multiple Offers

If you have multiple job offers, you can leverage them to negotiate a better deal. Politely inform each employer that you have other offers and that you are considering them carefully. This can prompt them to improve their offer to secure your acceptance. However, be honest and respectful in your communications to maintain a positive professional reputation.

The Long-Term Perspective

Remember, negotiation is not just about the immediate offer but your long-term career trajectory. A higher starting salary sets a baseline for future raises and bonuses. Accepting a lower offer may impact your earning potential for years to come.

However, it's also essential to consider the overall fit of the job. Sometimes, a role with a slightly lower salary but better growth opportunities, a healthier work-life balance, or a more supportive company culture can be more beneficial in the long run.

Negotiating a salary or contract is both an art and a science. It requires preparation, confidence, and strategic thinking. By understanding your worth, evaluating the total compensation package, having an unspoken range, choosing the right moment, listening actively, and being prepared for counteroffers, you can navigate this complex process successfully. Remember, every negotiation is an opportunity to advocate for yourself and set the stage for your future success. Embrace it with the seriousness and respect it deserves, and never underestimate your value.

Get a Coach

If you find salary negotiations particularly challenging, consider seeking professional help. Career coaches and mentors can provide valuable guidance and support. They can help you prepare, practice your negotiation skills, and offer feedback on your approach. Additionally, they can provide insider knowledge and tips specific to your industry.

Negotiating as a Woman or Minority

I was hesitant to include this in the book; however, research shows that women and minorities often face additional challenges in salary negotiations, including biases and stereotypes. If you fall into these categories, you must be even more prepared and confident in your negotiations. Arm yourself with data and be ready to advocate strongly for your worth.

Final Thoughts

Negotiating a salary or contract is a vital skill that can significantly impact your financial future and career satisfaction. By preparing thoroughly, understanding your value, and approaching the negotiation as a collaborative process, you can confidently navigate this challenging step. Remember that negotiation is not just about securing the highest possible salary but also creating a compensation package that reflects your worth and supports your professional and personal goals. With practice and perseverance, you can master the art of negotiation and set a strong foundation for your future success.

EIGHT

Accepting the Offer

The culmination of a job search journey is receiving an offer, a milestone that should fill you with a sense of pride and accomplishment. It's a moment that brings excitement, relief, and the promise of new opportunities. However, accepting a job offer involves more than saying "yes." It's a critical juncture that requires careful consideration, clear communication, and strategic planning. This chapter will guide you through the essential steps to ensure you make the best decision for your career and set yourself up for success in your new role.

Receiving the Offer

When you receive a job offer, your initial reaction may be one of elation. Take a moment to celebrate; this is a significant achievement. Whether the offer arrives via phone call, email, or formal letter, it's crucial to approach this moment with both enthusiasm and professionalism. It's highly recommended that you respond promptly to acknowledge the offer. Express your gratitude and excitement, even if you're not ready to decide. A simple email response could be:

"Thank you for extending the job offer for the [Position] role at [Company]. I am thrilled about the opportunity and appreciate your consideration. I want to review the offer in detail and will get back to you by [specific date].

Evaluating the Offer

Before you accept, take time to evaluate the offer thoroughly. Consider the following aspects:

Compensation and Benefits

Ensure the salary aligns with industry standards and your expectations. Does the offer meet what you expected during the negotiation process? When evaluating the offer, be sure to consider the total compensation package. Review the benefits package, including health insurance, retirement plans, bonuses, stock options, and other perks.

Job Responsibilities and Expectations

Revisit the job description and ensure it matches what was discussed during the interview. Understand your day-to-day responsibilities and performance expectations. Does the offer state what will be expected on your first day or first week?

Negotiating the Offer

Refer to Chapter 7 on "The Negotiation."

Making the Decision

The moment of truth arrives after negotiations conclude. You now have a revised job offer that reflects your discussions and adjustments. Taking a deliberate approach is crucial to ensure this decision aligns with your long-term career goals, personal values, and life circumstances.

Pray or Reflect on the Offer

Before finalizing your decision, spend some quiet time reflecting on the offer. Consider the following points:

Alignment with Career Goals: Consider how this position fits into your broader career trajectory. Does it offer the growth and learning opportunities you're seeking? Will it help you build the skills and experiences necessary for your future ambitions? Ensuring the job offer aligns with your long-term career goals is a key factor in making a decision that will benefit your professional development.

Personal Fulfillment: Assess whether the role will bring personal satisfaction and fulfillment beyond the professional benefits. Will the job be intellectually stimulating and enjoyable? Will it allow you to use your strengths and passions?

Life Circumstances: Consider how the job fits with your personal life. Will the work hours, location, and travel requirements align with your family, health, and personal commitments?

Seek Advice

If you are unsure, remember that seeking advice is not a sign of weakness but a way to gain clarity and confidence in your decision. It's a step that can make you feel supported and guided.

Mentors and Career Advisors: Trusted mentors or career advisors can offer seasoned perspectives based on their experiences. They can help you see potential opportunities and pitfalls that you might overlook.

Colleagues and Industry Peers: Those who work in the same industry can provide insights into the company's reputation, work environment, and growth prospects. They can also advise you on whether the offer meets industry standards.

Spouse, Family, and Friends: Discuss your offer and any concerns with your spouse if you are married. Be sure the two of you are aligned on goals for you and your family. Close family and friends are also a great resource to talk with. They know you well and can help you consider how the job aligns with your values and life goals. Their support and understanding of your circumstances can be invaluable.

Example Conversation with a Mentor: "Hi [Mentor's Name], I'm excited to share that I received a job offer from [Company]. Before making my final decision, I'd love to get your perspective on it. The role seems like a great fit for my skills and offers significant growth opportunities. However, I'm weighing it against the impact on my work-life balance and some uncertainties about the company culture. Any insights you have would be greatly appreciated."

Trust Your Instincts

While logical analysis and external advice are essential, your intuition plays a crucial role in decision-making. Trusting your instincts can make you feel empowered and confident in your choices.

Listen to Your Gut Feelings: If you feel uneasy or have lingering doubts, it's essential to address them. Investigate any concerns thoroughly, whether about the company's stability, the team dynamics, or the nature of the work. Conversely, a strong positive feeling can indicate that this opportunity is the right move for you.

Example Reflection: "After reviewing and discussing the offer with my spouse, coach, and mentor, I still feel uncertain about the company's commitment to work-life balance. My gut tells me to investigate their remote work policies and employee satisfaction. On the other hand, the prospect of leading a new project in a dynamic team excites me, which is a strong positive sign."

Conduct Additional Research

If there are still aspects you're uncertain about, you may need to do more research, which could help you decide. Reviewing the company's reviews using Glassdoor or LinkedIn can provide employee reviews and insights into the company culture, management style, and overall employee satisfaction. Reach out to current or former employees on professional networks. Their firsthand experiences can give you a clearer picture of what to expect. Understanding the company's financial stability can give you confidence in its long-term viability. Look at recent economic reports, news articles, and market performance.

Example Research Approach: "I decided to look up recent reviews of [Company] on Glassdoor and contacted a former employee I found on LinkedIn. The feedback was generally positive, but mixed reviews about the work-life balance. This additional information will help me weigh the pros and cons more accurately."

Balance Emotional and Rational Factors

Making a career decision often involves balancing emotional and rational considerations. On the emotional side, consider your passion for the role. Ask yourself if the job excites and inspires you. Cultural fit is another crucial emotional factor; envision whether you can thrive within the company's environment. Lastly, assess how the job will contribute to your happiness and personal satisfaction.

Rational factors also play a significant role in your decision-making process. Evaluate the salary and benefits to ensure they meet your financial needs and expectations. Consider the opportunities for career advancement, determining if the role offers clear paths for growth. Additionally, assess the company's stability and growth prospects to gauge job security. Balancing these emotional and rational factors can help you make a well-rounded and informed decision about accepting a job offer.

Example Decision-Making Balance: "I feel passionate about the projects I'd be working on at [Company], and I'm excited about the team's innovative approach. Rationally, the salary and benefits package is competitive, and the company is financially stable. Balancing these emotional and rational factors helps me feel confident about accepting the offer."

Make a Pros and Cons List

A simple yet effective tool is creating a pros and cons list. This visual aid helps you weigh the advantages and potential drawbacks of the job offer.

Example Pros and Cons List:

Pros	Cons
Competitive salary	Longer commute
Opportunities for advancement	Concerns about work-life balance
Positive company culture	Uncertainty about team dynamics
Comprehensive benefits package	Initial adjustment period
Exciting projects and responsibilities	

This structured approach can highlight which factors matter most to you and where potential compromises can be made.

Final Decision

After thorough reflection, seeking advice, and conducting additional research, you should feel well-prepared to make a well-informed decision. It's essential to cultivate a sense of confidence and clarity about your choice. This confidence reinforces your decision-making process and sets a positive tone as you prepare to embark on a new role.

Equally essential is ensuring you are fully ready to commit to the responsibilities and expectations of the new position. This readiness will facilitate a smooth transition and enable you to approach your new role with enthusiasm and determination from day one.

Formally Accepting the Offer

Once you decide to accept the offer, do so formally and graciously. Your acceptance should be professional and clear. Restate the key terms of the offer, express your gratitude, and convey your enthusiasm for joining the team.

Example Email: "Dear [Hiring Manager's Name],

I am delighted to formally accept the offer for the [Position] role at [Company]. Thank you for this opportunity and for addressing my requests during our negotiations. As discussed, my start date will be [specific date], with a starting salary of [agreed amount] and [any other negotiated terms].

I look forward to contributing to [Company] and collaborating with the team. Please let me know if any further steps or paperwork are required on my part before my start date.

Thank you once again for this opportunity.

Best regards, [Your Name]."

Resigning from Your Current Job

In chapter 10 we will discuss the recommended methods for resigning from your current job.

Preparing for Your New Role

With your acceptance confirmed and your resignation submitted, it's time to shift your attention toward preparing for your upcoming role. Organizing a smooth transition from your current responsibilities is crucial. Leaving your current job on a positive note demonstrates professionalism and courtesy, ensuring a seamless handover that minimizes disruption.

In addition to managing your transition, it's essential to mentally and practically prepare for your new position. Delve deeper into researching your new company, its culture, and the specifics of your role. This knowledge will help you acclimate more swiftly and understand the expectations of your new environment. Plan for your first day, considering logistical details such as commute routes, dress code expectations, and any initial tasks or meetings you want to prepare for.

Final Thoughts

Amidst the practical preparations, take a moment to acknowledge and celebrate your success. Starting a new job marks a significant milestone in your career journey. Celebrating this achievement recognizes your hard work and determination and sets a positive tone for the beginning of this new chapter.

Accepting a job offer is a pivotal moment that sets the stage for the next phase of your career. You can ensure a smooth transition and a strong start in your new role by carefully evaluating the offer, negotiating effectively, and preparing thoughtfully.

NINE

Handling Rejection

The journey of job hunting is often painted with a broad brush of optimism and ambition, yet the reality is far more complex. The path is rarely straightforward, frequently riddled with rejections, periods of eerie silence, and the frustration of receiving no feedback. These moments can be demoralizing, making you question your worth and abilities. However, it's crucial to understand that this is a shared experience, a rite of passage many have traversed. You are not alone in this. How you handle these setbacks can define not only your career trajectory but also your personal growth. Here's how to navigate this challenging landscape with resilience and grace.

Understanding Rejection: It's Not Personal

Rejection is perhaps the most direct form of feedback in the job search process. When you receive that dreaded "thank you for your application, but..." email, it's easy to take it personally. However, it's important to remember that rejection often reflects the fit for the specific role rather than your overall capabilities.

To cope with rejection, start by reframing your mindset. Shift your perspective from seeing rejection as a failure to viewing it as a learning opportunity. Each rejection brings you one step closer to the right fit. If possible, politely ask for feedback on your application or interview. Not every employer will respond, but when they do, their insights can be invaluable for your future applications. This proactive approach can empower you in your job search journey.

Celebrate the effort you put into the application process. Recognize the courage and hard work it takes to apply. Every application is a step forward, regardless of the outcome. This celebration of your effort can boost your morale and keep you motivated in your job search.

The Deafening Silence: Coping with No Response

The silence that sometimes follows after sending out applications can be one of the most unsettling aspects of job hunting. You might feel like you're shouting into the void, and the lack of acknowledgment can be disheartening. Automated responses, often received immediately after submitting an application, can add to this frustration. These automated replies typically confirm receipt of your application, mention that only shortlisted candidates will be contacted, or that you were not chosen without ever being contacted. While these messages can feel impersonal, they are a standard part of the process and not a reflection of your qualifications.

To maintain your momentum despite the silence, set realistic expectations. Understand that the hiring process can be lengthy and that employers receive hundreds, if not thousands, of applications. Delays are often not a reflection of your candidacy. Next, keep a job search log. Maintain a detailed record of all the jobs you've applied to, including dates and follow-up reminders. This helps you stay organized and proactive rather than feeling lost in the process.

Diversify your approach. Don't rely solely on online applications. Network with professionals in your field, attend industry events and leverage LinkedIn to connect with hiring managers. Sometimes, a personal connection can bypass the silence and open doors that would otherwise remain closed. By combining these strategies, you can navigate the job search more effectively and increase your chances of success.

Dealing with Zero Feedback: Turning a Negative into a Positive

When your application doesn't garner any feedback, it's easy to feel invisible. However, this situation can serve as an opportunity to refine your strategy and strengthen your applications.

Review your resume and revamp it if needed. Refer to Chapter 2, where we discuss what makes a strong resume. Tailor each application to the specific job by highlighting relevant skills and experiences. Ensure your documents are error-free, and consider seeking professional help to polish your resume.

Next, enhance your online presence. Make sure your LinkedIn

profile is up-to-date and reflective of your career aspirations. Engage with content related to your field, join groups, and share your insights to increase your visibility.

Finally, invest in skill development. Use this time to upskill by taking online courses, earning certifications, and attending workshops. These activities can enhance your resume and demonstrate your commitment to professional growth.

Ghosting or Rejection After Multiple Interviews

Handling ghosting or rejection after progressing through multiple stages of the interview process can be particularly disheartening. You've invested significant time and effort, and it's natural to feel disappointed or frustrated when the outcome isn't what you hoped for. However, this experience, though challenging, can also be a valuable learning opportunity.

First, give yourself permission to feel disappointed. Acknowledge your emotions rather than suppressing them. This is a normal and healthy part of the process. After a brief period of reflection, try to shift your focus to the positives. Recognize the progress you made by reaching the advanced stages of the interview process. This indicates that your qualifications and skills are strong and you were seriously considered for the position. Use this as a confidence booster for future applications.

If you've been ghosted after multiple interview rounds, consider following up with a polite and concise email to your contact at the company. Express your continued interest in the position and inquire about any updates. Sometimes, a nudge can prompt a response, providing closure or reigniting the conversation. If you receive no reply, moving forward without dwelling on the lack of communication is crucial.

When you do receive a rejection, if feedback is not provided, don't hesitate to request it. Constructive feedback can offer valuable insights into areas for improvement and help you refine your approach for future opportunities. Remember, each interview experience is a stepping stone toward the right job. Stay resilient, maintain your momentum, and keep refining your strategy. The right opportunity will come, and your perseverance will pay off.

Building Resilience: The Long-Term Game

The emotional toll of job hunting can't be underestimated. Building resilience is essential to withstand the inevitable ups and downs. To fortify your mental and emotional well-being, start by practicing self-care. Regular exercise, a balanced diet, adequate sleep, and mindfulness practices like meditation can significantly impact your mood and energy levels.

Next, seek support. Don't isolate yourself; talk to friends, family, or a career coach about your struggles. Sometimes, just sharing your experience can lighten the load. Lastly, stay positive and persistent. Celebrate small victories, whether a well-crafted cover letter or a successful networking conversation. Remember, persistence is key! The right opportunity is out there, and your continued efforts will eventually pay off.

The Power of Reflection: Learning and Growing

Every application, interview, and interaction is an opportunity to learn and grow. Reflect on your experiences regularly to gain valuable insights. Start by identifying patterns. Notice any recurring themes in rejections or feedback. Are there skills you need to develop? Is there a common weakness in your applications?

Next, set goals based on your reflections. Establish specific, actionable objectives for improvement. This could include enhancing a particular skill, expanding your network, or refining your job search strategy. Finally, stay adaptable. The job market is dynamic, so be willing to adjust your approach based on what you learn and the feedback you receive. This flexibility can significantly improve your chances of success.

Final Thoughts

Handling rejections, zero feedback, and no response in the job hunt requires resilience, adaptability, and a proactive mindset. Remember, each step, whether successful or not, is part of a larger journey towards finding the right fit for your skills and aspirations. Keep pushing forward, stay positive, and trust that your efforts will lead you to the opportunity you deserve.

TEN

Graceful Exit

Leaving a company, whether voluntarily, due to termination, or because of a layoff, can be a challenging experience. However, handling this transition with grace and professionalism can significantly impact your future career opportunities and personal well-being. This chapter explores the best practices for exiting a company, highlighting the importance of maintaining a positive attitude and avoiding the pitfalls of publicly criticizing your former employer.

Voluntary Departure

When leaving a company voluntarily, providing sufficient notice is a mark of professionalism. The standard notice period is usually two weeks, but it may vary depending on your role and company policies. Proper notice lets your employer plan for your departure and find a suitable replacement. This gesture is courteous and ensures that you leave on good terms, making it more likely that your employer will provide a positive reference in the future.

Creating a transition plan demonstrates your commitment to ensuring a smooth handover of your responsibilities. Document your tasks, ongoing projects, and critical contacts. Offer to train your successor or team members to fill the gap your departure will create. This proactive approach shows that you care about the well-being of the team and the company, which can leave a lasting positive impression on your colleagues and supervisors.

An exit interview is an opportunity to provide constructive feedback about your experience at the company. Approach this conversation honestly but tactfully, focusing on areas for improvement rather than personal grievances. This can help the company enhance its work environment for future employees. You can contribute to positive organizational changes by providing balanced feedback, potentially benefiting your former colleagues and future employees.

Termination

Being terminated can be a blow to your confidence and morale. However, maintaining professionalism and composure is crucial. Reacting negatively can damage your reputation and future job prospects. Instead, seek to understand the reasons behind the termination and learn from the experience. Accepting responsibility, if applicable, and showing a willingness to improve can turn a negative situation into a valuable learning experience.

Requesting feedback from your employer to gain insight into the factors leading to your termination is a powerful tool for personal growth and future success. This information can be invaluable for personal growth and for avoiding similar issues in the future. Understanding the specific reasons for your termination can help you identify areas where you need to improve, making you a stronger candidate for future opportunities.

While termination can be a setback, it also presents an opportunity to reassess your career goals and explore new paths. Update your resume, network with industry contacts, and consider additional training or certifications to enhance your skills. Use this time to reflect on what you truly want in your career and take steps toward achieving those goals. By turning a termination into an opportunity for growth, you can emerge from the experience stronger and more focused.

Layoffs

Layoffs are often beyond your control and can happen for various reasons, including economic downturns or company restructuring. However, maintaining a positive attitude and demonstrating resilience during this period is essential. Employers and recruiters are more likely to respond favorably to candidates who demonstrate resilience and optimism. Showcasing your ability to stay positive in the face of adversity can set you apart from other candidates.

Many companies offer support resources for laid-off employees, such as career counseling, resume workshops, and job placement services. Take advantage of these offerings to ease your transition into a new role. These resources can provide valuable assistance in finding a new job and can help you refine your job search strategy.

Networking is crucial when searching for new opportunities. Reach out to former colleagues, attend industry events, and engage with professional groups on social media platforms like LinkedIn. Building and maintaining a solid professional network can open doors to new opportunities and provide support during your job search. Networking can also help you stay informed about industry trends and job openings, increasing your chances of finding a suitable position.

The Power of a Positive Attitude

Your attitude during your departure can significantly impact your reputation. A positive, professional approach leaves a lasting impression on your former employer and colleagues, who may become valuable references or networking contacts in the future. Demonstrating professionalism and positivity can help you maintain strong relationships and can lead to future job opportunities or collaborations.

Maintaining a positive attitude is not just about managing stress; it's about fostering a sense of optimism and hope for your future. Dwelling on negative experiences can lead to bitterness and hinder your ability to move forward. By focusing on the positive aspects of your experience and looking forward to new opportunities, you can maintain a healthy mindset and stay motivated during your job search.

Employers value candidates who can handle difficult situations with grace. Demonstrating a positive attitude during a job interview, despite a challenging departure from a previous company, can set you apart from other candidates. Showcasing your ability to remain positive and professional in the face of adversity can make you a more attractive candidate to potential employers.

The Pitfalls of Public Criticism

In the age of social media, it can be tempting to vent frustrations online. However, publicly criticizing your former employer can have serious consequences. Potential employers often review your social media profiles; negative comments can damage your professional image. Maintaining a professional online presence is crucial for your career prospects.

Publicly disparaging your former employer may lead to legal repercussions, especially if your comments are defamatory. It's essential to be mindful of the legal implications of your online activity. Avoiding negative remarks about your former employer can help you avoid potential legal issues and maintain a positive professional reputation.

Your professional network is a valuable asset. Negative comments about a former employer can alienate you from industry peers and reduce your opportunities for future collaborations or job referrals. Maintaining positive relationships within your professional network can provide support and open doors to new opportunities. By staying positive and professional, you can build a strong reputation that will benefit you throughout your career.

Final Thoughts

Regardless of the circumstances, leaving a company is a significant life event that requires careful handling. Maintaining a positive attitude, providing constructive feedback, and avoiding public criticism can ensure a graceful exit that preserves your professional reputation and opens doors to future opportunities. Remember, every end is a new beginning, and how you handle your departure can set the tone for the next chapter of your career. Embrace the change with optimism and professionalism, and you will be better positioned for success in your future endeavors.

www.ingramcontent.com/pod-product-compliance
Lightning Source LLC
Chambersburg PA
CBHW072053230526
45479CB00010B/851